THE
SIBERIAN
DEADFALL

A survival trap used by woodsmen of the Russian Taiga.

DROPSToNE PRESS
Pocket Field Guide: The Siberian Deadfall
Creek Stewart

Copyright © 2016 by Creek Stewart
All Rights Reserved

Copyeditor: Jacob Perry

All rights reserved. No part of this book may be reproduced in any form by any means without express permission of the author. This includes reprints, excerpts, photocopying, recording or any future means of reproducing text.

If you would like to do any of the above, please seek permission first by contacting us at http://www.dropstonepress.com

Wholesale inquiries please visit http://www.dropstonepress.com
Purchase this Pocket Field Guide and others in this series at
http://www.creekstewart.com

Published by DROPSToNE PRESS
ISBN 978-0-9976906-5-1

This book is presented solely for educational and entertainment purposes. While best efforts have been used in preparing this book, the author and publisher make no representations or warranties of any kind and assume no liabilities of any kind with respect to the accuracy or completeness of the contents and specifically disclaim any implied warranties of merchantability or fitness of use for a particular purpose. Neither the author nor the publisher shall be held liable or responsible to any person or entity with respect to any loss or incidental or consequential damages caused, or alleged to have been caused, directly or indirectly, by the information or skills contained herein. Every person is different and the advice and strategies contained herein may not be suitable for your situation. The story and its characters and entities are fictional. Any likeness to actual persons, either living or dead, is strictly coincidental.

dropstonepress.com

INTRODUCTION

The Siberian Deadfall is almost as elusive as the quarry it is designed to capture – the Russian Sable. The Sable is a species of Marten whose fur is highly prized by trappers in the subarctic coniferous forests of the Siberian Taiga. Use of the Siberian Deadfall to catch Sable dates back to at least the 17th century and is still used today by isolated trappers in that cold, harsh region of the world. Any trap design that has been used by professional trappers for hundreds of years to survive in one of the most unforgiving landscapes on the planet is worth studying.

While designed to capture and kill Sable, the Siberian Deadfall can just as well be used to secure a variety of wild game in any survival scenario, including but not limited to squirrel, chipmunk, raccoon, opossum, skunk, mink, and rat. The three-piece carved trigger system is an ingenious design that can be quickly mastered. This Pocket Field Guide will cover every detail you need to know about carving, setting, and being successful with the Siberian Deadfall of the Russian Taiga.

WHEN TO USE THE SIBERIAN DEADFALL

While the three-piece trigger can be carved very quickly at base camp, a traditional Siberian Deadfall site can take some time to prepare. Unlike most deadfalls, the Siberian Deadfall is raised off the ground and consists of two parallel beams that run horizontally and are held in place by two upright tree stumps or staked poles.

The Siberian Deadfall platform (*detailed in the next section*) can take up to 30 minutes to build. Because of this time investment, the Siberian Deadfall is a trap that should be used when a survivor is expecting to stay in the same area for at least a few days, or longer. For best results, a traditional trap-line of 12 to 40 Siberian Deadfalls that are roughly 100 to 200 yards apart should be made. All trap-lines should be checked at least every few days to gather game and/or reset triggered traps.

BUILDING THE DEADFALL PLATFORM

The entire deadfall platform is typically created from two trees that are 2" to 4" in diameter and growing roughly 6' to 10' apart. These trees should be as straight as possible. Tall, straight spruces are used almost exclusively in the Siberian Taiga and are perfectly suited for the task. After locating the two trees, each one should be cut with a saw or axe approximately 48" to 60" inches from the ground.

Next, 2" wide by 12" tall notches must be cut into the center top of both remaining tree stumps (*as shown in the diagram*). This is easily done with a quality 36" bow saw, but it can also be accomplished with an axe if a bow saw is unavailable. It is important that the notches be carved smoothly and are absent of splinters, bumps, and rough areas.

The top and bottom pieces (*called planks*) of the deadfall trap
are made from the straight upper trunks of the two trees whose
stumps have been notched. Cut two straight sections that are
each 2' longer than the distance between the two stumps.

The bottom plank of the deadfall must be placed first. Both
ends of this plank should be thinned out on each side so they
slide into the notches on the top of each stump. Don't thin the
sides so much that the plank wobbles within the notches. Each
end should fit snugly. Once placed across the two stump notches
the plank should be as level as possible. Adjustments in the
notches may need to be made at this point. Once the bottom
plank is level, no further modifications will need to be made.

Now, it's time to place the top plank (*the second straight tree trunk*). Again, both ends of this plank should be thinned out on each side. This top plank, however, should slide freely into the notches. It must be able to slide up and down each notch easily, without sticking or hanging up. I've found that a 1/4" gap between the plank and the notch walls is about perfect (*1/8" on each side*).

Once the above steps are accomplished, the deadfall platform is finished. Now, let's explore how to carve the trigger system.

THE SIBERIAN DEADFALL CARVED TRIGGER

The three-piece Siberian Deadfall trigger is comprised of two upright, mated components and one notched bait stick. This sensitive trigger system is placed between the upper and lower deadfall planks and is held together by tension caused by the weight of the upper deadfall plank. When the bait stick is disturbed, the trigger sticks collapse, causing the upper plank to fall on and trap the animal.

The carved trigger starts with a single piece of wood that is approximately 1" wide x 1/2" thick x 8" long.

Start by cutting a 60-degree angle at the top and bottom of the stick *(as shown in the diagram)*. The top and bottom should not be a sharp chisel tip but rather flat and blunt.

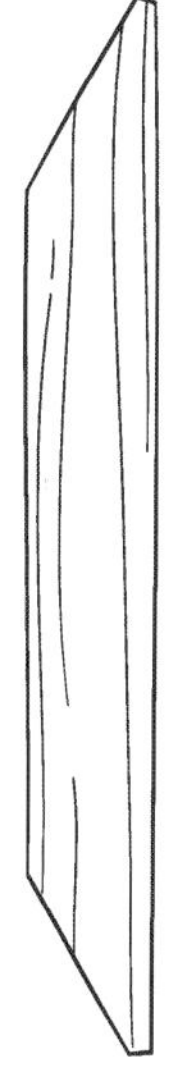

Next, measure up 2" from the bottom right hand side of the trigger stick and make a saw cut exactly half way through (*as shown*). I prefer to use a saw but this can also be done with a knife.

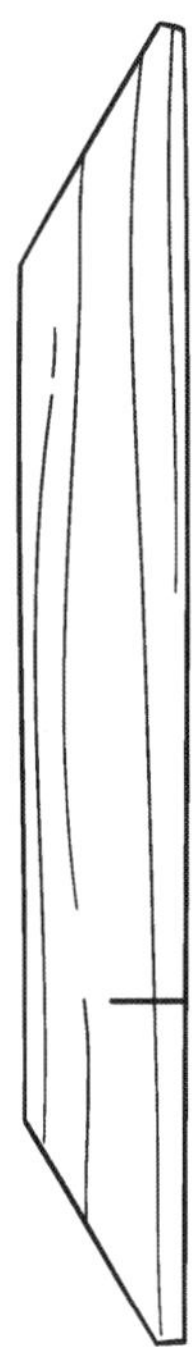

Then, again using a saw or knife, carve out a chunk of wood at a 60-degree angle above the saw cut from the previous step. This new notch will resemble a number 7.

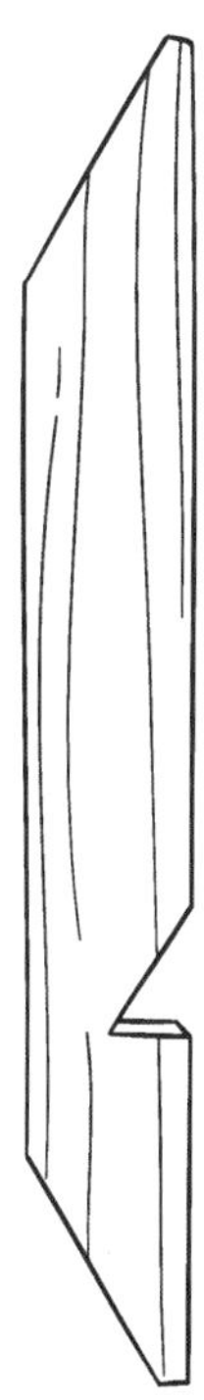

Lastly, place your knife blade across the middle of the trigger stick *(as shown)* and push it down to split the stick in half all the way to the number 7 notch. You may have to hit the back of your knife blade with a stout stick *(called batoning)* to start the split but it should not be difficult.

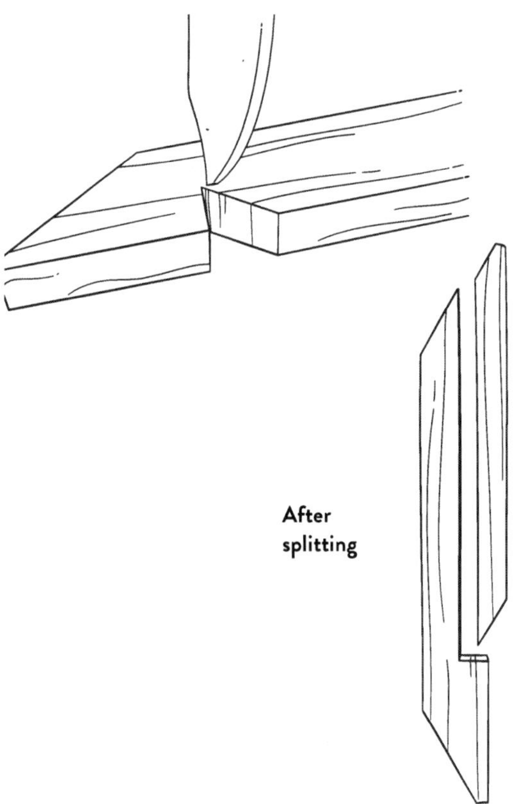

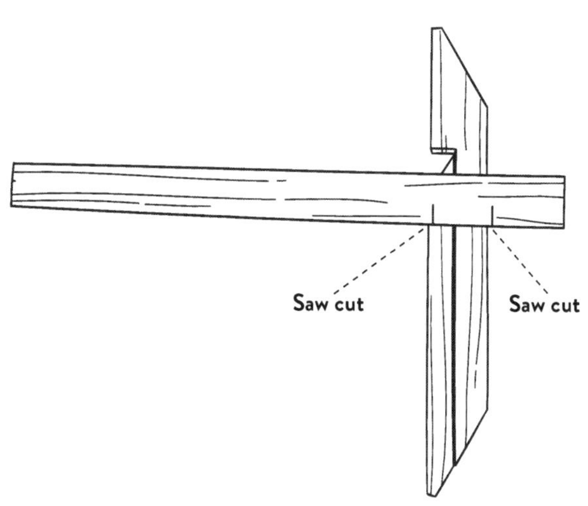

Once the trigger stick is split, you are ready to notch the bait stick which is designed to hold these two trigger sticks together. The bait stick should be 6" to 8" in length and can be round or rectangular. If round, it should be no larger than 1/2" in diameter. If rectangular as shown, it should be approximately 1/2" thick by 1" wide. Start by making two saw cuts about 1/4" deep that are the exact width apart as the two trigger sticks sandwiched together, as detailed in the diagram.

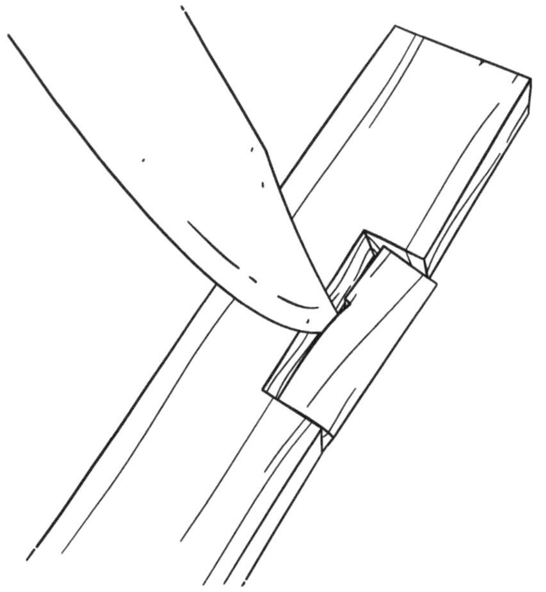

Once the two saw cuts are made, the interior can be easily chipped out with a twisting motion using the tip of your knife blade.

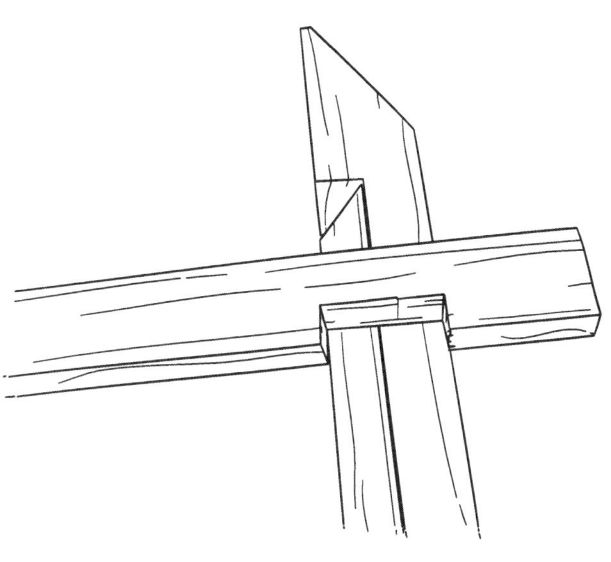

The end result should be a rectangular notch in the bait stick that is about 1/4" deep and is as long as the width of the two trigger sticks.

This notch prevents the trigger sticks from collapsing under the pressure of the top plank. Once the bait stick is disturbed and the trigger sticks are freed from the carved notch, the deadfall collapses.

Above is a close up diagram of the trigger sticks set between the top and bottom planks. Notice how the bait stick prevents them from collapsing.

BAITING THE DEADFALL

Unlike most other deadfall sets, the bait on the Siberian Deadfall is actually offset from underneath the top deadfall plank. This positioning forces the animal to turn sideways on the lower plank and reach for the bait, which makes for a far more effective trapping position that is perpendicular to the plank. The trigger system is placed at approximately 1/3rd of the way along the bottom plank in either direction.

Before setting the trigger sticks, bait should first be fastened to the bait stick. Forest birds, fish, meat chunks or scraps of fur are all excellent bait choices for both carnivorous and omnivorous animals. Nuts, berries and peanut butter are preferred choices for squirrel and other herbivores. Regardless what is used, bait should be fastened securely to the bait stick with string or wire. It can also be pushed into a split in the stick if extra string or wire isn't available for tying. The bait should be secured approximately 2" to 4" from the two upright trigger sticks along the bait stick. This seems to be a good distance for most game.

To set the deadfall, first lift one side of the top plank and rest it on the top of the notched tree stump. Then, holding the two mated trigger sticks together with one hand (*as shown*), place the top plank on top of them to apply pressure to the trigger. While still holding the mated trigger sticks together, gently place the bait stick with your other hand and slowly allow the triggers sticks to collapse under the pressure of the top plank. The notch in the notched bait stick will prevent them from collapsing completely and the trap will be set until the bait stick is disturbed.

BUILDING THE ROOF

A roof over the bait stick and trigger system serves multiple purposes. First, it protects your bait. Especially during heavy snowfall, the roof prevents your bait from being covered and hidden by snow. The roof also adds weight to the top plank for a faster, more humane kill when the trigger is tripped. The roof is very easy to construct and begins with a long limb leaned across the top plank on each side of the bait stick. Then, pine, spruce, or other branches are placed across these diagonal poles to form a roof over the bait stick as shown.

PREVENTING LOST TRIGGERS

I've seen trigger sticks jettison up to 20 feet away from the trap platform when the trap collapses. In thick brush or heavy snow, it's not hard to imagine that these small carved sticks could become lost. A wise trapper will use an 8" length of thin thread or fishing line to tie each piece to the next. This simple trick will prevent the trigger pieces from disappearing when the trap collapses without affecting the trap's function.

CONCLUSION

Although its origin is in the subarctic forest of Russia, the Siberian Deadfall design and trigger system is versatile enough to be used in almost any environment. While front-loaded with a little more time and energy than some other more popular survival deadfalls, it is a trap design that has stood the test of time by some of the most seasoned trappers in the world. Its effectiveness and simplicity of manufacture place the Siberian Deadfall on the short list of survival traps every outdoorsman or woman must know.

Siberian Deadfall carving kits are available at *http://www.creekstewart.com*. These kits include one finished trigger system and the blank wooden pieces to carve your own and master this deadfall at home.

Remember, it's not IF *but* WHEN,
CREEK

NOTES:

NOTES:

NOTES:

NOTES:

Made in the USA
Middletown, DE
12 April 2023

28629252R00018